W9-AMU-853

Elaine St. James's

Little Guide to
LIVING SIMPLY

**Andrews McMeel
Publishing**

Kansas City

ISBN: 0-7407-0084-7

Library of Congress Catalog Card Number:
99-60672

Illustrations by Julie Herren

Be selective about giving out
your E-mail address.

Never remodel.

If you must remodel, resist
the urge to live in your home
while it's being remodeled.

Think twice before going into
business with a friend.

Leave your shoes
at the front door
when you come into
the house.

If you get rid of 50 percent of
the clutter you have in your life
you'll still have too much—
but you'll only have half as
much to organize.

If you ever need something
you've gotten rid of, you can
always get it again. If you
can't get it again, it won't be
the end of the world.

Stop trying to
change people.

Develop a deep rapport
with nature.

Realize that you don't *have*
to work ten hours a day,
you just *think* you do.

Realize that you *can* stop
working ten-hour days, it
just *feels* as if you can't.

For the next thirty days quit work an hour earlier than you usually do; when the thirty days are up, keep doing it.

Arrange your life so you can
do the work you love to do.

Replace your lawn with a
beautiful, low-maintenance,
drought-tolerant ground cover
that never needs to be mowed.

Know that you don't
have to do it all,
you just *think* you do.

Always sit down to eat.

Eat slowly and savor
every bite.

Leave the TV off for
thirty days; when the
thirty days are up,
do it again.

Avoid long, boring
office meetings.

Create beauty in your life.

Never allow a phone call
to interrupt a meal
with your family.

Stop being a perfectionist.

Avoid trade shows.

Never borrow money
from a friend.

Never loan money to friends;
give it to them instead.

Cancel subscriptions
to the magazines you
don't have time to read.

Take your next vacation
at home.

Know yourself.

Be yourself.

Don't buy clothes that have
to be hand-laundered.

Learn to delight in solitude.

Create an electronic-free zone
in the mornings: no TV, no
radios, no Walkmans, no CDs,
no video games, no computers,
no telephone.

Teach yourself to do only
one thing at a time.

Get rid of all but one or two
of your credit cards.

Use a credit card only
if you pay the balance in full
by the end of the month.

Laugh out loud at least
once a day.

Do what you can to make your
relationships work; if you can't
make them work, move on
from them gracefully.

If you're always in a frantic
rush to get out of the house
on time in the morning,
get up half an hour earlier.

Never, ever go into debt for
something you put under a
Christmas tree.

For the next thirty days don't
buy *anything* but food and
absolute necessities; when the
thirty days are up, do it again.

Train yourself to stop
responding like Pavlov's dog to
a ringing phone.

Draw names for your family
Christmas gift exchange.

Cherish silence.

If you don't have the money to
pay for it in full by the end of
the month, don't buy it.

Teach your kids that if they
don't have the money on hand,
they can't afford it.

If you're in debt, do whatever
you have to do to get out.

Arrange your life so you don't
have to commute to work.

Make sure you have time every
day to do nothing.

Never go shopping
without a list.

Take at least five minutes each
day to think about your life.

If there's something in your life
you're not happy with,
change it.

Whenever you request a
mail-order catalog, ask that
your name, address, and
phone number not be sold
to other catalog houses
or phone solicitors.

When you receive an
unsolicited piece of junk mail,
write "please remove this
name from your list" on the
address card, put everything
back into the postage paid
envelope, and return it
to the sender.

Get rid of the exercise
equipment you never use and
take a brisk thirty-minute walk
five times a week.

Resist the temptation to move
to a bigger house.

If it's not working,
stop doing it.

Live by this uncluttering rule:
If you haven't used it in a year,
pass it on to someone
who can.

Whenever you agree to do
something, estimate the
amount of time it will take,
then double your estimate.

Figure out when to speak up
and when to keep quiet.

If call waiting drives you nuts,
cancel it.

Learn to trust that still, small
voice within.

Say no to every request
for your time for the next
thirty days. When the
thirty days are up, do it again.

Understand that the more
you say no, the easier it gets.

Arrange your schedule so you
get all the sleep you need.

Always drive within
the posted speed limit.

Establish this simple
household rule for your kids:
You lose it, you find it.

Avoid traveling
over the holidays.

Realize that most of what you
think matters doesn't matter as
much as you think it does.

Avoid garage sales.

Stop buying clothes you have
to take to the dry cleaners.

Avoid shopping malls.

Never sue anyone.

When you go on vacation
don't leave a number where
your office can reach you.